7.90

John F. Kennedy
and the Stormy Sea

by Howard Goldsmith

Illustrated by

Renné Benoit

Aladdin

New York   London   Toronto   Sydney

To Michelle Sapers, with love
—H. G.

For my parents
—R. B.

❦

ALADDIN PAPERBACKS
An imprint of Simon & Schuster Children's Publishing Division
1230 Avenue of the Americas, New York, NY 10020
Text copyright © 2006 by Howard Goldsmith
Illustrations copyright © 2006 by Renné Benoit

Designed by Lisa Vega
The text of this book was set in 18-Point Century Old Style.
Manufactured in the United States of America
First Aladdin Paperbacks edition January 2006
2 4 6 8 10 9 7 5 3
Cataloging and publication data is available from the Library of Congress.
ISBN-13: 978-0-689-86816-0   ISBN-10: 0-689-86816-2 (Aladdin pbk.)
ISBN-13: 978-0-689-86817-7   ISBN-10: 0-689-86817-0 (Aladdin library edition)
LCCN 200593182

John F. Kennedy
and the Stormy Sea

John F. Kennedy and his
ten-year-old sister, Kathleen,
were digging for clams on the beach.
John called his sister Kick.
She called him Jack.

"I am tired of digging for clams!"
Kick said. "I want to have some fun."
Jack looked out at the
clear blue water of the bay.
"All right, let's go sailing,"
Jack said.

"Where to?" Kick asked.

"Nowhere special," Jack said.

"Wherever the wind takes us."

"But, Jack, you know we always
need to tell Mother and Father when
we take a boat out," Kick said.

"Mother and Father went into town,"
Jack said. "You are being such a
worrywart. What if we take
the boat over to Osterville?
There we can stop and tell
Father's friend Captain Manley
that we are sailing."

"All right," Kick said.

They moved out into the bay.

Soon they reached Captain Manley.

"Jack," the captain said,

"you brought the boat into harbor

like a real sailor!"

"Thank you," Jack said.

"We came to tell you that

Kick and I are going for a sail."

Captain Manley looked up at the sky.

"Those clouds look mean," he said.

"They are storm clouds.

If I were you, I would not go

too far out."

"Okay," Jack said.

Jack and Kick sailed out of the harbor.

The waves slowly grew larger.

Soon they were beating against the boat

like angry fists.

Then, without warning,

a thick fog rolled in.

Jack could not see land.

13

Kick started crying.

She grabbed one of Jack's arms

and would not let go.

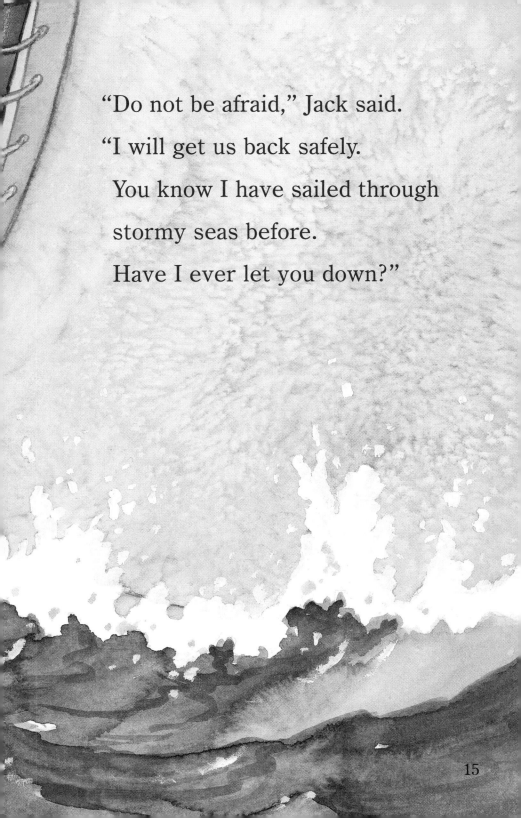

"Do not be afraid," Jack said.

"I will get us back safely.

You know I have sailed through

stormy seas before.

Have I ever let you down?"

"No," Kick said,

still hugging Jack's arm tightly.

She smiled bravely,

but her lower lip shook.

For Jack there was no time
to be scared.
The boat was rocking
up and down in the water.
Jack gripped the wheel
with both hands.

At the back of Jack's mind

he heard his father's words:

"Trust yourself, Jack.

You have what it takes."

Jack kept steering through the fog.

Back on land, Jack's father and
older brother, Joe,
watched the tall waves
crash against the beach.

They both knew that
Jack was a good sailor.
"Jack has brought that boat in
a thousand times!" Joe said.
"Yes, and in worse weather,"
his father said.

Still, his voice was
tight with worry.
Jack was just a boy.

A few hours later
Father took action.
"We have waited too long,"
he said. "I will ask
the Coast Guard to search
for them."
He ran toward the house.

"Wait, Father!" Joe called.

"Look!"

He pointed toward the water.

A small sailboat

cut through the fog.

It sailed straight up to the dock.

Jack and Kick were waving

from the deck.

Jack tied the boat to the dock.

He helped Kick off the boat.

Kick raced into her father's arms,

but Jack walked up to him

as calm as a clam.

"A bit foggy out there," he said.

"But not a problem."

"Great job, my boy!" said Jack's father.

"I am proud of you.

You always do your best."

"You are my hero, Jack!" Kick said.

Father led the children

back up to the house.

When he grew up
Jack joined the U.S. Navy.
He became a captain.

One night during World War II

his boat was sunk by

a Japanese ship.

Many men fell into the sea.

But Jack was brave

and a strong swimmer.

He saved the sailors from drowning.

For his courage and leadership

Jack won a gold medal.

He returned home a national hero.

Later John F. Kennedy became a United States senator. Then, in 1960, his dream of becoming president of the United States came true.

Here is a timeline of John F. Kennedy's life:

1917	John Fitzgerald Kennedy is born on May 29, in Brookline, Massachusetts
1927	Kennedy family moves to Riverdale, New York
1931	Enters his freshman year at the Choate School
1940	Graduates from Harvard University
1941	Enlists in the U.S. Navy
1943	Kennedy's boat, PT 109, is sunk by a Japanese ship. Kennedy rescues injured crewmen
1944	Receives the Navy and Marine Corps Medal for "extremely heroic conduct"
1946–53	Serves in the U.S. Congress
1953	Marries Jacqueline Bouvier
1953–61	Serves in the U.S. Senate
1957	Daughter, Caroline Bouvier Kennedy, is born
1957	Kennedy is awarded Pulitzer Prize for his book, *Profiles in Courage*
1960	Elected President of the United States
1960	Son, John F. Kennedy Jr., is born
1961	Establishes the Peace Corps
1962	Forces U.S.S.R. to remove missiles from Cuba
1963	Assassinated in Dallas, Texas